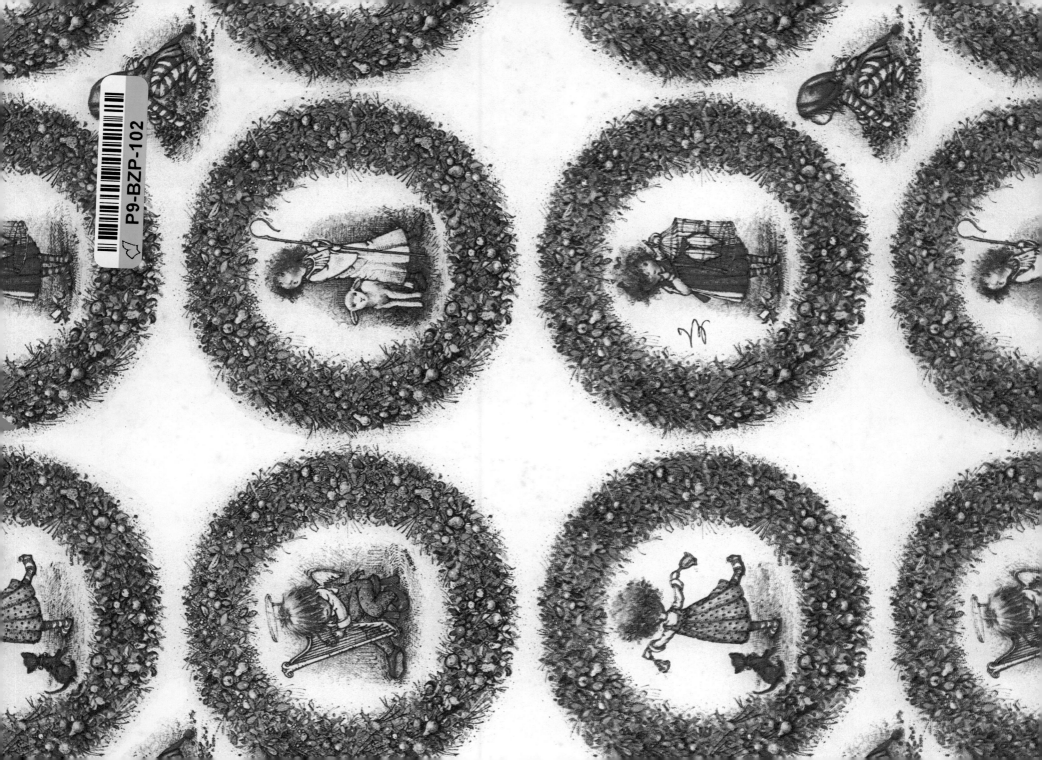

A Merry Christmas To:

From:

THE
NIGHT BEFORE
CHRISTMAS

Written by:
Clement C. Moore

Illustrated by:
Holly Hobbie

Platt & Munk Publishers / New York
A DIVISION OF GROSSET & DUNLAP

'Twas the night before Christmas, when all through the house

Not a creature was stirring,
not even a mouse;

The stockings were hung by the
chimney with care,
In hopes that St. Nicholas soon
would be there.

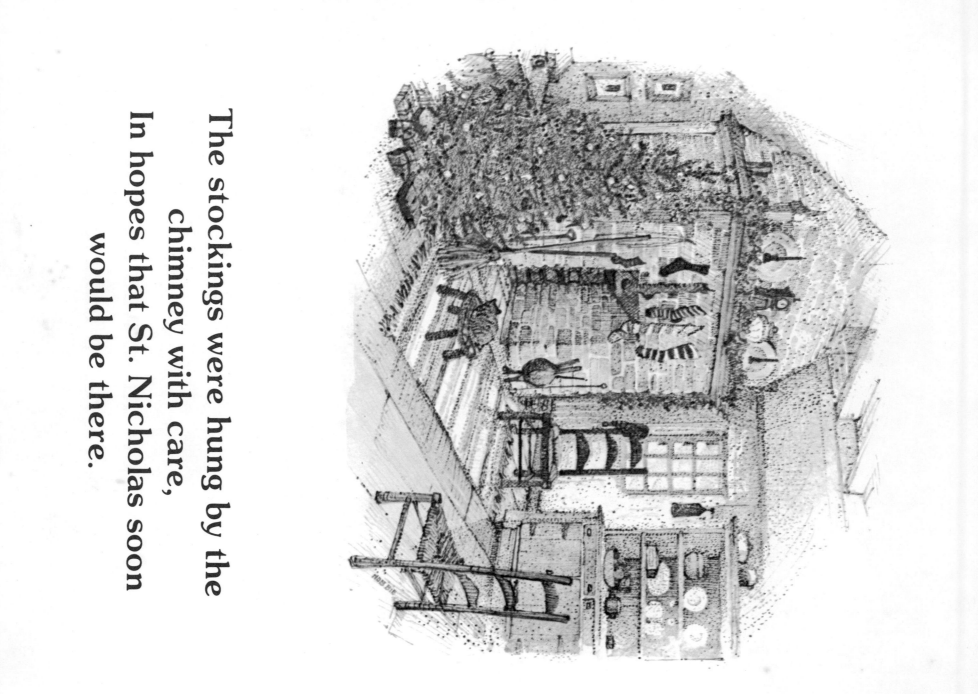

The children were nestled all snug
in their beds,
While visions of sugar-plums danced
in their heads;

And mama in her kerchief, and I in my cap,
Had just settled down for a long
winter's nap -

When out on the lawn there arose
such a clatter,
I sprang from my bed to see what
was the matter.
Away to the window I flew like a flash,
Tore open the shutters and threw up
the sash.

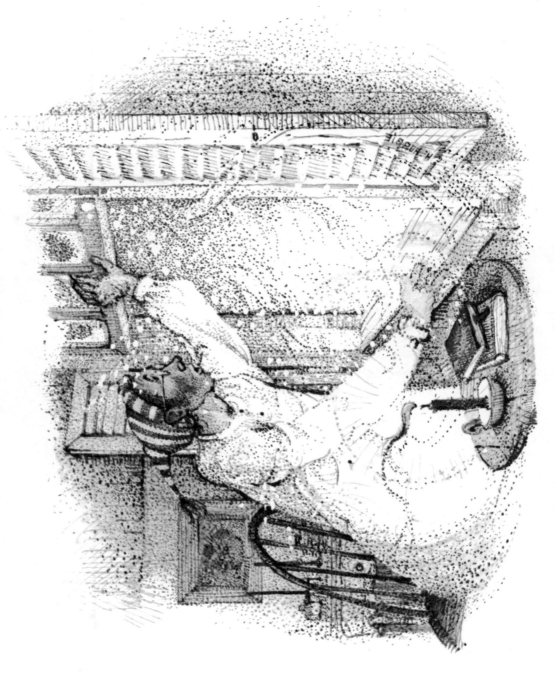

The moon, on the breast of the new-
fallen snow,
Gave a luster of mid-day to objects below;
When, what to my wondering eyes
should appear
But a miniature sleigh, and eight
tiny reindeer,

With a little old driver, so lively and quick,
I knew in a moment it must be St. Nick.

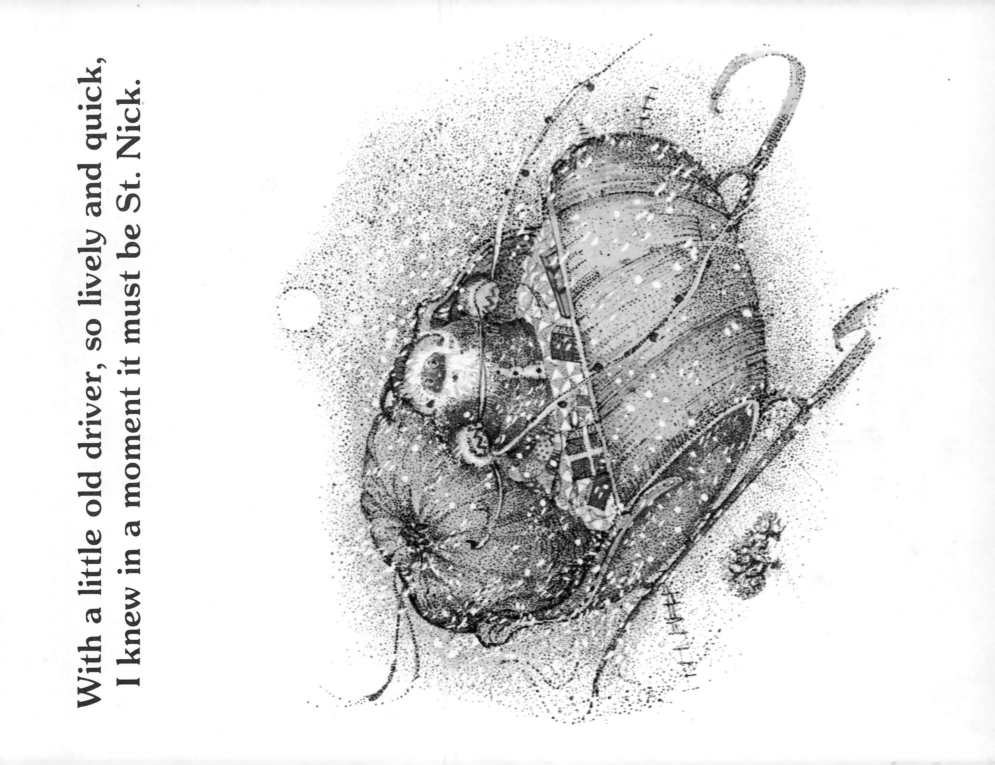

More rapid than eagles
his coursers they came,
And he whistled, and shouted
and called them by name:

"Now, Dasher! now, Dancer!
now, Prancer and Vixen!
On, Comet! on, Cupid!
on Donder and Blitzen!
To the top of the porch!
to the top of the wall!
Now, dash away, dash away,
dash away, all!"

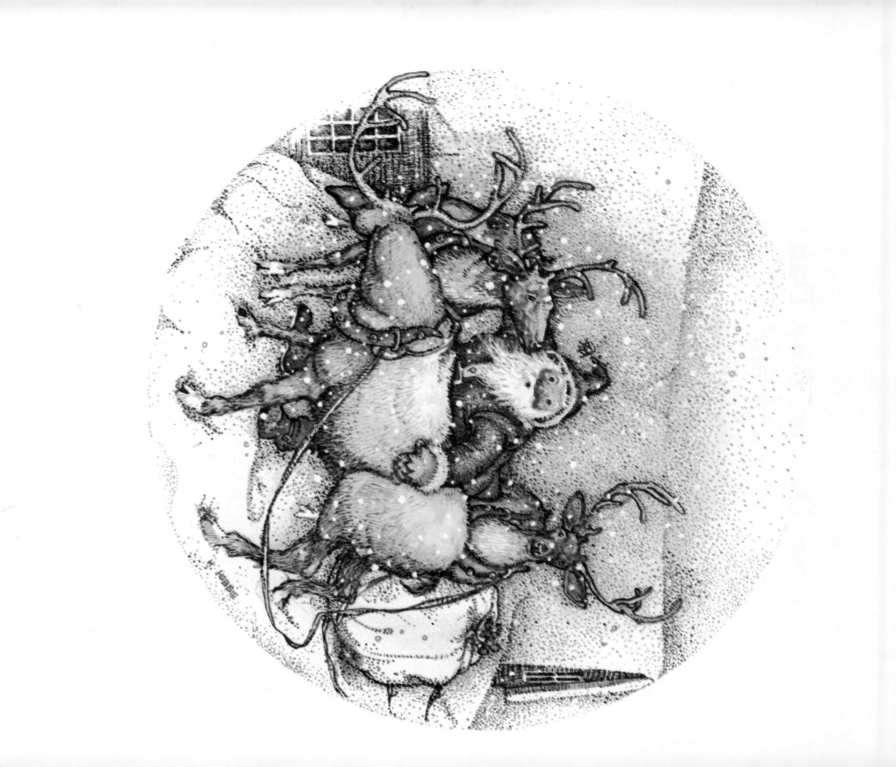

As dry leaves that before the
wild hurricane fly,
When they meet with an obstacle,
mount to the sky,
So, up to the house-top the coursers
they flew,
With a sleigh full of toys - and
St. Nicholas, too.

And then in a twinkling, I heard on the roof
The prancing and pawing of each little hoof.
As I drew in my head, and was
turning around,
Down the chimney St. Nicholas came
with a bound.

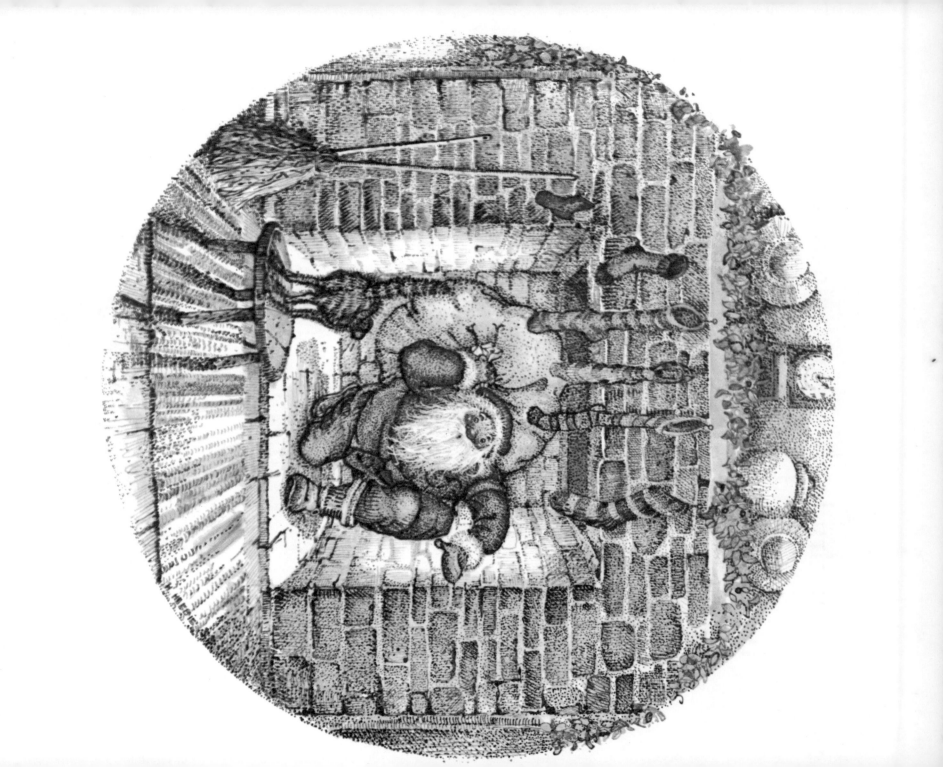

He was dressed all in fur from his
head to his foot,
And his clothes were all tarnished
with ashes and soot.
A bundle of toys
he had flung on his back,
And he looked like a peddler
just opening his pack.

His eyes how they twinkled! His dimples
how merry!
His cheeks were like roses, his nose
like a cherry.

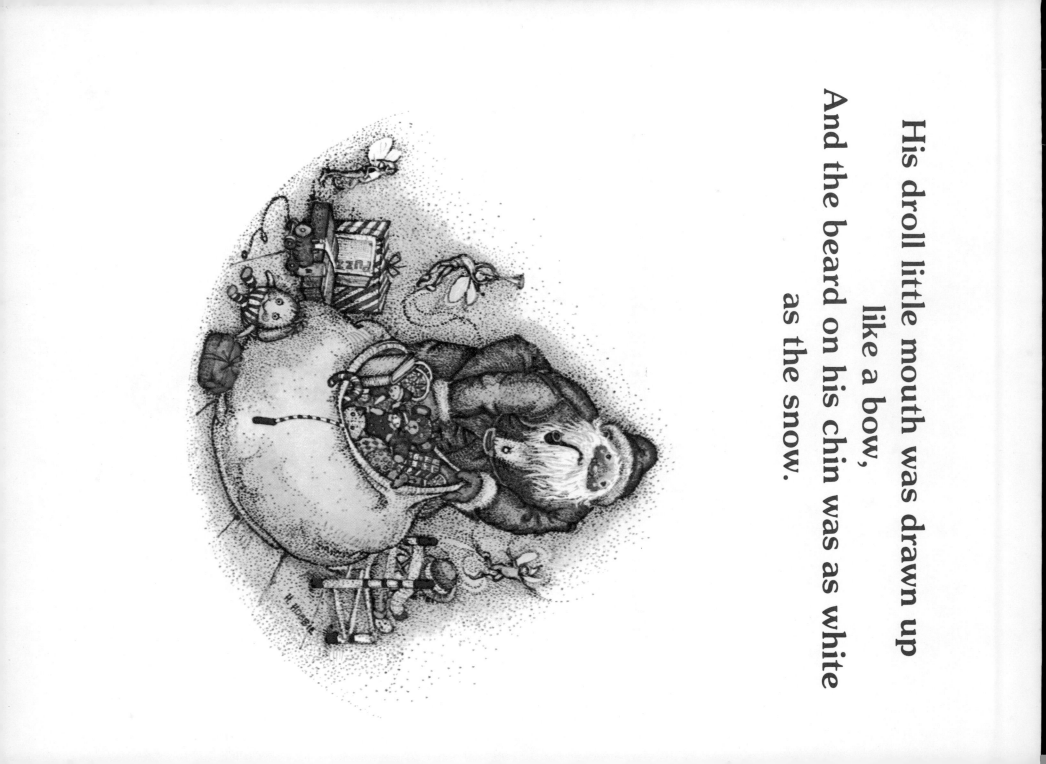

His droll little mouth was drawn up
like a bow,
And the beard on his chin was as white
as the snow.

The stump of a pipe he held tight in his teeth,
And the smoke it encircled his head
like a wreath.
He had a broad face and a little round belly
That shook when he laughed, like a
bowl full of jelly.

He was chubby and plump - a right
jolly old elf —
And I laughed when I saw him,
in spite of myself.
A wink of his eye, and a twist of his head,
Soon gave me to know I had nothing
to dread.

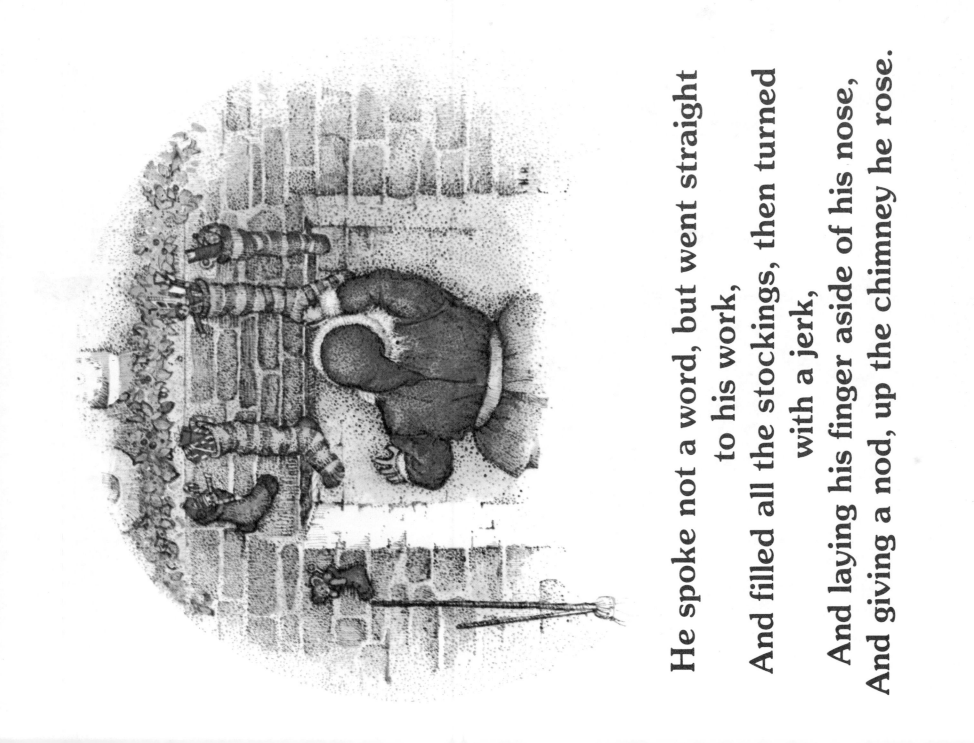

He spoke not a word, but went straight
    to his work,
And filled all the stockings, then turned
    with a jerk,
And laying his finger aside of his nose,
And giving a nod, up the chimney he rose.

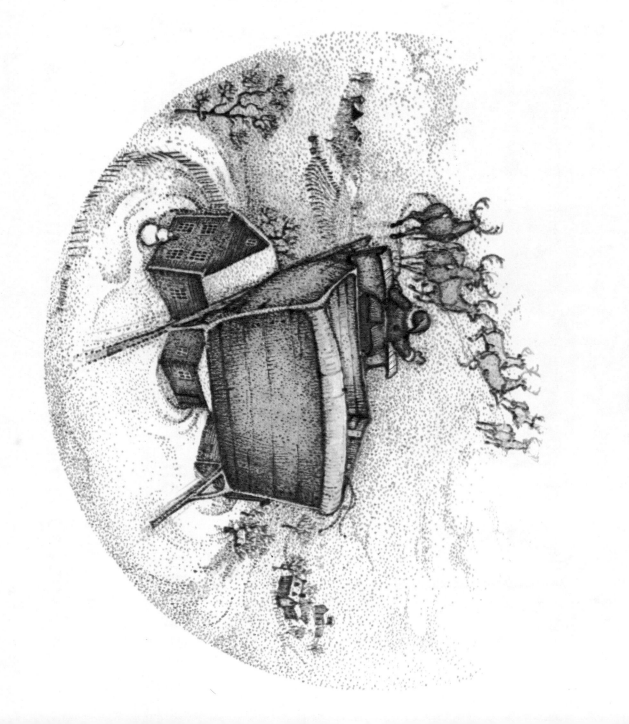

He sprang to his sleigh, to his team
gave a whistle,
And away they all flew like the down
of a thistle,
But I heard him exclaim as he drove
out of sight,

"Happy Christmas to all,
and to all a good night!"

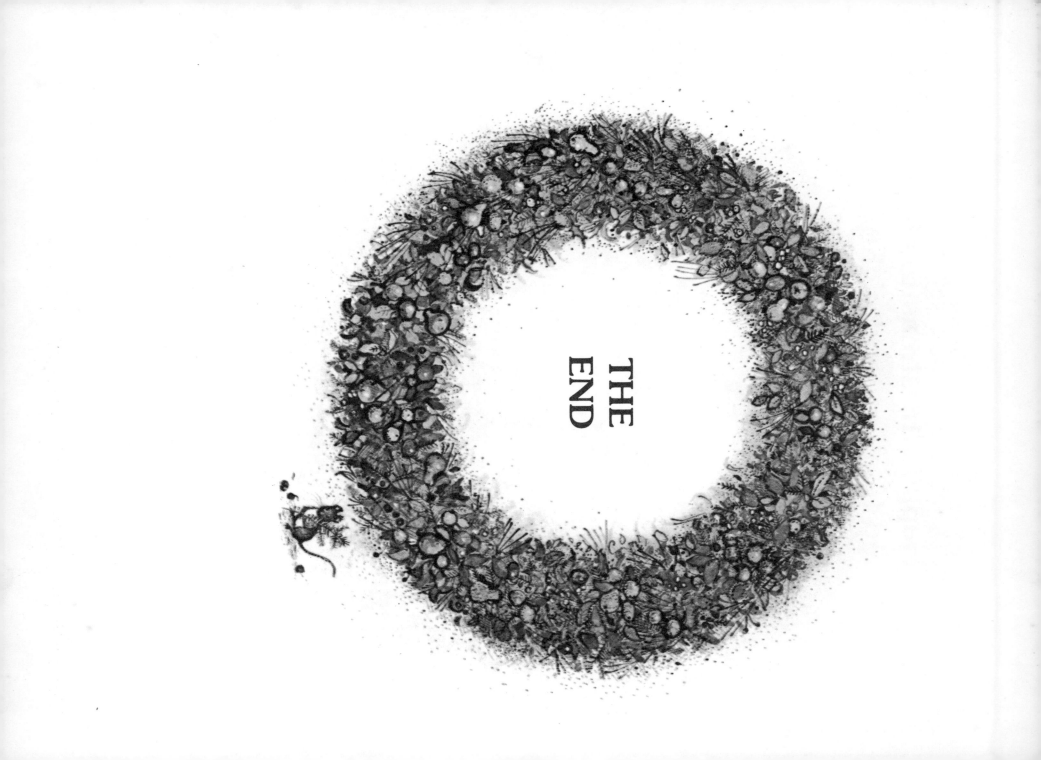

THE
END